Gun T RPO
4.0 New Addition

Introduction

 # Introduction

I, like most coaches, have worked hard to listen to people I respect and attempt to take little nuggets from those willing to give. Now, I have been given the opportunity to give back and I hope this offensive system can be of help to you in your journey as a coach. Feel free to take any part of this offense that can help you, but I feel what makes it work is the entire system.

We have worked hard to continue to grow it and work through the problems that can come from blending different worlds.

The entire system can be found here:

Introduction

This is version 4.0 of the Gun T RPO system. For those of you who may not be familiar with my situation, I developed this system while at Southside Batesville, a 4A school in Arkansas from 2016-2019. Ran it one season at Searcy, AR a 6A school and returned in 2021 to Southside. In 2022, I took the head football position again at Southside.

Each stop has had a different QB, and different athletes and the system will always center around the talent the school provides. Each school and year has talent, but it varies often at the high school level. It has been my goal to work to create a system that has answers for each group. This season we were much different than in 2021.

"Never stop growing as a coach" - I love the thrill of learning and studying football, almost as much as actually coaching the game. When you feel you have nothing new to learn, I'd recommend you find a new profession. The passion we must bring with us is what our athletes deserve from us.

There is no magic pill. When we watch the game of football there are champions that run a variety of offensive systems. I would point out that those who seem to have the most success have a belief in their offense. Most have worked hard to go over as many "if-then" situations and build in answers. I am no different. I wanted to create an offense that would work against any coverage, any front or any blitz package the defense might throw at us. While the game is won and lost with the players on the field, I wanted to be sure to give my players every advantage I could.

Recommendations

 # Quotes

"Coach Simpson shows how you can evolve your system to fit your personnel. Too often coaches will as Coach Simpson put it "try to pound the square peg in the round hole." Coach's system is one of the best I have seen in my 30 years of coaching, Gun-T 2.0 is an evolution of the system that shows the versatility to adapt to the ever changing kids we see at the high school level." – Matt Bartley

"As a first year head coach and a first time offensive play caller, I don't know where we would have been without the material that coach Simpson has available. We went from 4-6 to 7-4, to the third round of the postseason, and earned the second best record in school history. The program hadn't been to, nor won a playoff game since 2015. Thank you coach Simpson."
-Mike Granato, Head Football Coach, West Orange High School, Florida

"I've been following coach Simpson for a while now and it's very clear to me that even though I may not be a HC, we have similar philosophies. If you are a Wing T guy looking for ways to "Modernize" your offense, or a Spread guy looking for an effective and efficient run game this is the offense you should be looking at!" Coach Sheffer

"The Gun T RPO System really helped us evolve our wing T offense and really put defenses in conflict. This system helped us break a 20 game losing streak and finish with a winning record for the first time since 2014."
-Tom Mulligan, Head Coach Elmwood Park High School, Elmwood Park, New Jersey

"Coach Simpson has modernized the under center Wing-T offense through RPOs, Tempo and outside the box thinking into the explosive Gun-T offense. His courses and books break down the offense into digestible chunks and provide the answers to the most frequent problems you will encounter while running the offense. Coach Simpson is also a class act and is always willing to help out."
-Will Theobold, OC/OL Park High School, Cottage Grove, MN

"Coach Simpson does an awesome job explaining his system, and he does it a way that people like myself who are not familiar with RPOs can understand!" Coach Coleman

Quotes

"Coach Simpson does a phenomenal job of teaching this dynamic system. He starts from the foundation and works his way through in detail. Coach Simpson give you the details; yet keeps it simple and efficient just like his offense." - Lucas Stanton

"Over the past year, I have purchased a number of items from Coach Simpson ranging from books to coaching materials. I couldn't be more satisfied with the content and detail of these items. Coach Simpson is a forward thinker and an innovator in this game. Whether you are a young coach or a seasoned veteran there is something for everyone."
-Mike Kloes, Offensive Line Coach, Wahama High School

"Wanting to add modern shotgun style play to your Wing-T system? Coach Simpson has created the definitive playbook combining classic Wing-T elements with modern spread RPO philosophies. A must buy for any Wing-T coach looking to expand their repertoire."
-Tim Jacobs, Head Football Coach, Rex Putnam High School, Milwaukie, Oregon

Table of Contents

Acknowledgments

 # Acknowledgements

When I became a football coach many years ago, I wanted to study the game as much as possible. I was very fortunate to have several coaches that served as mentors throughout my career. I also found several coaches that were putting out information before it became "normal". I am thankful for all the guys that were willing to put their system out there.

I started my career as a huge Tony Franklin fan. Then I moved to Rick Stewart about 7-years ago. I wanted to blend these systems. But these coaches, as well as several others, were the pioneers. I want to thank all these coaches who guided me along the path.

I also want to thank those coaches I have worked with during my time at Madison Academy, Alabama Christian Academy, Southside and Searcy. Coaches are only as good as their staff and I have been part of some great ones and now am leading another very talented staff.

I'd like to also thank my administrations I've had the honor of serving in my career. These jobs are often as thankless as coaching jobs!

Coaches also recognize that the players are the key to the game and I have been blessed to coach some of the finest young men in the country. The relationships I have with them are more precious than any win. Coaching is a hard, demanding, but truly rewarding profession.

Most importantly my family has been the rock that has always been there for me. My children are now becoming young adults and it is flying by. My wife has been my #1 supporter since day 1. She has been through 0-10 and been through championships and she has never wavered.

Theory

Theory

I like to start each book with the theory behind our offense as I feel we need to know why this offense can work and what makes it tick.

The Gun T RPO system is the best of 3 worlds:

The Wing-T offensive system has been around for many years. The best part of the Wing-T is the run game that utilizes angles and takes advantage of the defensive alignment by creating them. The Wing-T is also known for its "series" based offense, which has multiple plays that look the same in the backfield action.

The RPO system has taken football by storm over the last couple of decades. To be able to place defenders in "conflict" with the run/pass option game gives the offense a numbers advantage at all times. This system is also great because while it seems the quarterback must make a decision on each play, it also "shrinks" his world by having him read only one or two defenders.

The Power-Spread game is gaining steam throughout every level of football. To be in the shotgun, but still have a downhill running game is deadly and difficult to defend. Utilizing tight ends and H-backs has become "new" again in football. The reality is this system has been around for awhile, just not in the shotgun.

When combined into the Gun T RPO system, these worlds at first seem at odds with one another. However, after a deeper dig, these offenses are all concept based that build in answers to handle any defense that may show up on a given day.

This entire offense is based on answering the "If-Then" question that must be answered. A good defense will have multiple problems it presents to the offense and your system must have built in answers. Hopefully, through reading some of this material it may provide answers.

Theory

R.P.O. stands for Run-Pass-Option.

In this offense the "R" comes first. We are trying to protect our base run game by supplying answers to problems. The RPO portion of the offense is to build-in answers to protect the running game.

This offense has 1st/2nd/3rd level RPO's. My suggestion to those of you new to this portion of the game would be to start with 1st level RPO's, slowly progress to 2nd, and then possibly 3rd level RPO's.

The beauty of the RPO game is that you can attach the SAME RPO concepts to the entire running game series. Once the quarterback learns the read he can work it on buck sweep or strong belly.

Each of our RPO's is built to address problem areas. We want to have very quick concepts we can go to in the middle of a game. The RPO section is put in with Buck Sweep and Strong Belly and will give you simple RPO concepts that affect the lowest amount of players (generally the quick tackle and backside players). This allows the offense to become very good at the base run plays with minimal time spent on the backside adjustments.

Calling Plays

 # Calling Plays

Play call from the coach to the players will follow this format:

1- Formation (+any tags)
2 - Any motion/shift
3 - Run Concept (+any tags)
4 - RPO Play side
5 - RPO Backside

These can get wordy if you run multiple movements and RPO's on each side, but many plays can be just three words. The only player who needs to learn the entire call is the quarterback.

*As you can see throughout this playbook it will be filled with our base run and pass concepts. But you can be as creative as possible. If I listed every possibility this playbook could easily be well over 400-pages.

Play call examples –

Red – Buck – Bubble
We would be in "red" formation. The run play would be "buck" and the RPO would be "bubble".

Red – Lion – Belly – Fast
Formation would be "red-lion" (or trips). Run play would be "belly" and the RPO/Screen would be "fast screen".

Red – Empty – Fly – Buck – Bubble
Formation would be Red-Empty. Motion would be "fly" or F motion. Run play would be "buck" and the RPO would be bubble screen.

*More of these play calls are available in the Gun-T-RPO playbook

Personnel

Personnel Choices

When running this offense there are a few "non-negotiable" parts you absolutely must have. But most of the time there are player with the required skills at each position. As I mentioned in a prior chapter, as coaches we must adapt our offense to the players we have. That being said there are a few qualities you should search for at each position.

Quarterback - This is the key to your offense. Ideally, this position would be a dual threat. While not everyone has that option, he must be at least able to pull the ball from time to time at the vary least. The offense will drastically adapt to his skill set. If he is a thrower, it has multiple passing schemes/play action and of course RPO plays. If he is a runner there are several designed runs for him and the ability to go Empty is a must in today's game.

In short, find your best athlete if possible, that can handle the pressure of playing QB and adapt to what he does well. If given the option, I've always deferred to the guy that can run the ball and use his legs over a traditional QB. However, you can be successful with both.

F - This should be your best athlete. By design this position will touch the ball the most of any spot (except the QB position). It is easy to get them the ball in space (empty/screens) or simply run the ball (buck/belly). As with every position, you must adapt to their skill set, but this needs to be your best player.

B - This is the hardest position to find and the most important one. It will cause you to adjust what you do offensively to fit his skill set. I attempt to find your second-best player if he is able/willing to block and put him in this position. Size will matter at this spot, since he will be asked to down block defensive ends and linebackers. If he is gritty, but undersized there are some adjustments that can be made, but he must be effective blocking.

The second part of his job is as important. We want this player to be a good runner – if he is very athletic, we will run jet and counter with him. He also needs to be able to catch at least short passes or play action passes. In my opinion, other than the QB, this position will dictate how much you use certain formations and plays.

 # Personnel Choices

A – A traditional slot WR. Often for us this is our third RB or an undersized WR. Can get him the ball on multiple concepts and even hand him the ball if you need to.

X – Traditional WR. Depending on what you have available this position can be utilized often, or not much.

Y – Tight-end. Must be able to block defensive lineman. His job is crucial on buck. We generally pick our 3rd guard for this spot. If he has the ability to catch the ball that is great, but he must be a willing and able blocker for this offense to work.

QG – Most important lineman on the team. He needs to be your most athletic player on the line. Size is secondary. He will be pulling on almost all strong side runs. When you decide who goes where, start at this position.

SG – Second most important lineman on the team. He will pull kick most of the time, but needs to be athletic enough to wrap for Quick Belly. Usually the stronger, not as athletic of the two guards.

QT – Next most important lineman. What his skill set brings to the table will allow you (or not) to run to the quick side and all your RPO game on the backside. He also needs to be able to get in space on screen and get to second level on RPO game.

C – Must be very consistent at snapping for the offense to run smoothly. Usually this is a smart kid that can call the fronts and is able to handle backside blocking. If he is not as great a blocker, we can give help, but if he is a solid blocker it makes the scheme much easier to achieve.

ST – Usually this is a very physical, but not as athletic tackle. Often for us this is our biggest lineman. If he played at the college level he would have to play guard since often these types of bodies struggle with speed. Must be able to down block, double team and cut/hinge on backside runs.

New Concepts

New Concepts

As with any offense, the Gun T System must continually evolve to have answers for new problems the defense will throw at it. While the base offense and concepts are a perfectly fine and can easily be a stand alone look, these new concepts will be a great addition to the offense.

I do want to caution, that adding in new concepts to a system that is not well run yet, is a recipe for disaster. Be sure to be great at the "meat and potatoes", or base plays, before venturing too far into adding new concepts. These are solid concepts and can help, but they must fit with your personnel and not detract from the base offensive system.

The goal of any new concept should be to build on the base of what the offense can do, or to take advantage of how defenses are set to stop the base offensive plays. We do not EVER want to add a play into our offense that does not build on a concept we already have in our offense or is an inexpensive install. Adding new plays too often can be a recipe for disaster for many offenses.

The main concerns we have with anything new and the questions we ask, before installing it:

1) Does this fit with our offensive structure? Can we use this one concept off another main concept or build in complements?
2) How expensive an install is this? How much time must be dedicated to this concept in practice and how often do we anticipate using it in a game?
3) Does this fit our players? Can our players perform this concept against all our opponents or most of them?

If we answer all of these questions and like our responses, we go forward with the install. If we feel it will take time, we must cut something else out of our playbook for that season. There are only so many hours in the day and reps at practice to be great at a concept.

Jet

We have run "Jet" for a few seasons, but this year we added in an orbit motion – "Boat" and ran this as a quick pitch. This was from the "Faster than the fly" series from Blair Hubbard.

The idea for us was that this sets up our orbit motion run game off of this look, as well as the play hitting much quicker to the edge.

While we do still run it off the speed motion, this has become a nice addition to our offense.

We also run our entire "Jet series" off the "boat", or orbit, motion from our B. This allows us to keep the same look to the defense and run our roll out pass game and complimentary runs.

Jet

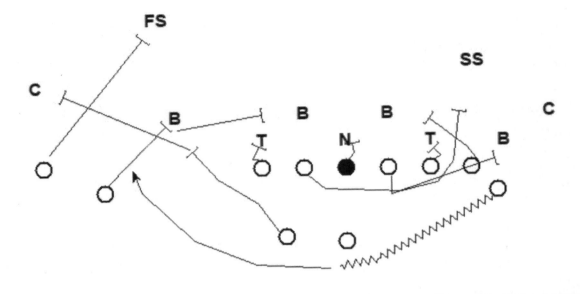

Position	Alignment
X	Cracks first second level defender inside
A	Cracks first second level defender inside
F	Work to OLB if he stunts, if not, work to the corner
Y	Block for buck
B	Orbit – "boat" – motion behind QB at FULL Speed. Read block of F.
QT	Reach the DE
QG	Block for buck
C	Reach the nose
SG	Block for buck
ST	Block for buck
Q	Pitches – like a basketball toss. Snap ball as "B" nears back hip.

This is a frame by frame shot of our team running jet with our "boat" motion from our B-back. The first picture shows our base "red" formation.

This picture shows the motion of the back and the snap of the ball. We want the ball snapped as the B is not quite to to QB.

The QB now has the ball and the B should be FULL SPEED. The QB will then PUSH the ball with two hands.

*This is taken from Blair Hubbard's "Faster than the Fly" system.

This is how far we pitch the ball to the back. We are now much wider than normal and do not have to block the 4-technique.

Boat – Jet

FS

SS

C

B

B

B

C

T

N

T

B

This is "boat" motion with our Jet Sweep. We made this an automatic "joker", or guards away, call. This helped us identify who was reading what key on our offense.

Because the pitch hit so wide, we didn't feel the need to account for any defensive player inside the Quick Guard. And using a false pull, set up our other plays on offense.

We also taught our slot WR to block the OLB, but if he stunted, to work to the ILB. The "F" was taught to assume the OLB needed to be blocked, and then work to whatever was outside of him.

Boat-Boot

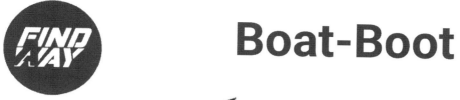

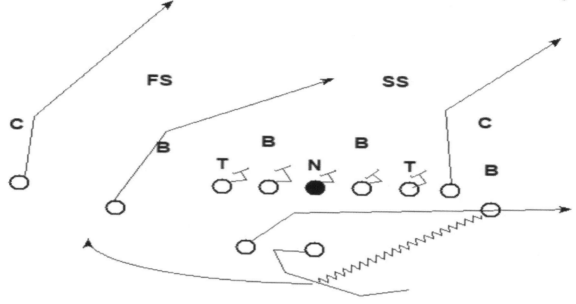

Position	Alignment
X	Skinny post or "win" route – get inside leverage on the corner
A	Crossing route – working to 12-15 yards – goal is to make safety cover us
F	Get into the flats – we are the hot route on this concept
Y	Corner route
B	Fake the jet off "boat" motion
QT	Rodeo/Lasso
QG	Rodeo/Lasso
C	Rodeo/Lasso
SG	Rodeo/Lasso
ST	Rodeo/Lasso
Q	Fake the jet and boot right – hot route is the "F"

Boat – Boot

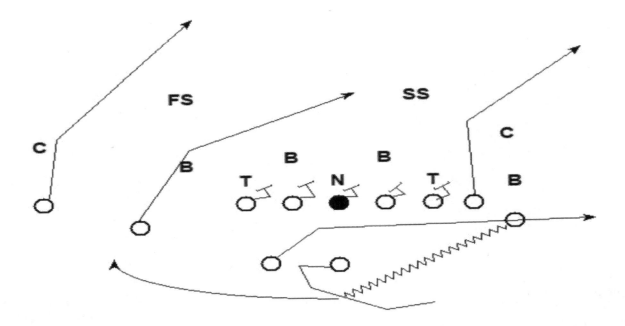

This is the compliment to the "Jet" play. It can also be run with flat motion, but works much better with timing off the pitch look.

The QB read is simple –

1) Pressure in the face should throw the "F" in the flats
2) Cornerback bites, throw the TE
3) Can read backside FS also on the Dig/Post combination

QB footwork is to fake the two pitch and boot back to the strong side. This is a "rodeo" protection to the right and "lasso" to the left.

Boat Motion

We can run our entire "Jet-series" from this type of motion if this is how we would run our Jet Sweep look. That would include all the following plays:

- Quick Belly
- Buck/Trojan/Belly back to the strong side
- Draw
- All our roll out concepts (The "B" would run a bubble instead of a chute route

While this motion has been a good one for us, we can also run our normal "Bus" motion if we are going to run our Quick Belly Read game or want to use RPO's.

In summary, I'd recommend the "Boat" motion if you have a more traditional QB and the "Bus" motion if you have a better athlete or RPO player.

A-Throwback

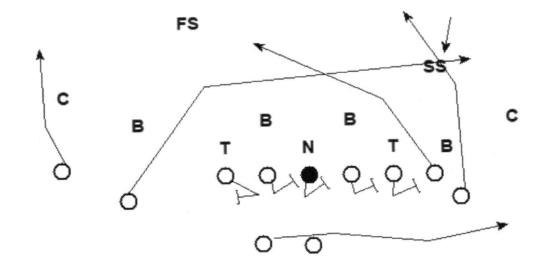

Position	Alignment
X	Outside release – Go route
A	Working across the field 15-18 yards
F	Swing route to the strong side
Y	Dig/Post – must occupy the safety
B	Skinny Post – Win Route
QT	Pass Pro
QG	Pass Pro
C	Pass Pro
SG	Pass Pro
ST	Pass Pro
Q	Reads the DB that is playing deep over the TE/Wing – F is checkdown

A Throwback

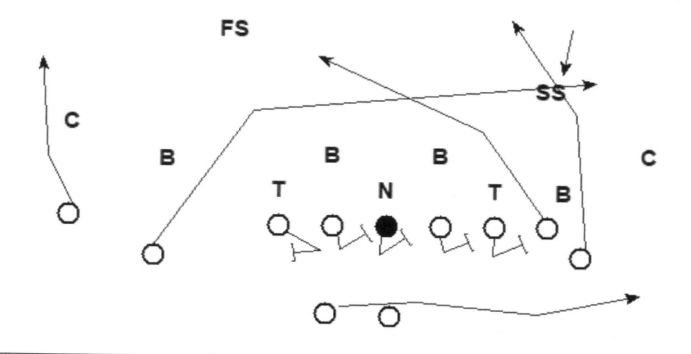

We have a few flavors of this pass concept. The most common one is off our motion game.

However, if we have a pocket passer and want to run a simple version without rolling out we can run it this way.

The QB read is the DB that is playing deep. If he takes the "B" on the skinny post we should be able to throw the "A" on the 15-18 yard cross 99% of the time. It he stays home, the skinny post should be open as the "Y" will run directly at the other safety and occupy him.

Our "F" becomes the route we throw if the corner also bails in coverage to help on the deeper routes.

Bus - A Throwback

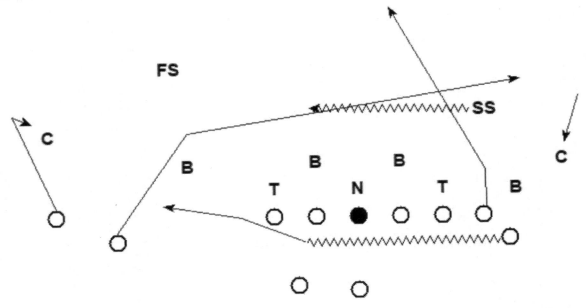

We worked this concept to teams that were rolling coverage to our motion. The QB read's the corner for the TE skinny to the crossing route.

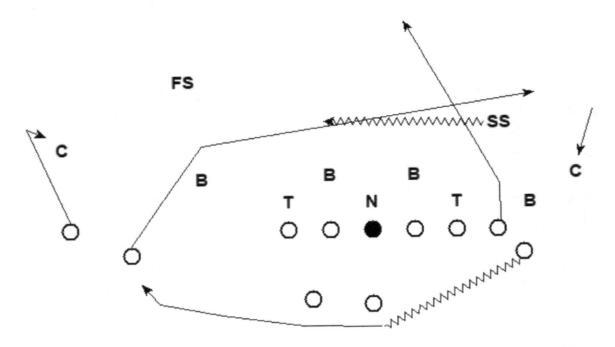

This is the same play off our "boat" motion. We usually would run both motions to see the reaction of the defensive secondary and then decide which motion to use. The read is the same for the QB.

Rail

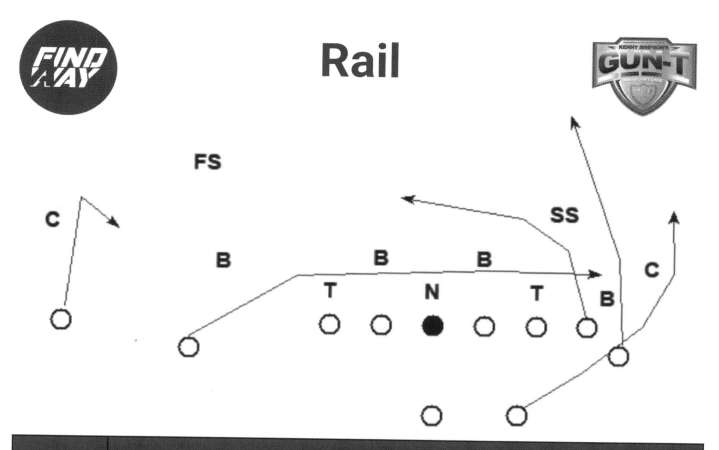

Position	Alignment
X	Choice Route or Hitch – This player is dead on this play, so the coach can choose
A	Shallow route – get across the formation quickly
F	Rail Route – get vertical and wide as quickly as possible
Y	Drag route – same as he runs on Waggle
B	Skinny Post or "Win" route. Work to get vertical inside the cornerback
QT	Pass Pro
QG	Pass Pro
C	Pass Pro
SG	Pass Pro
ST	Pass Pro
Q	Reads the corner – Rail to skinny – If all are covered find the shallow

Rail

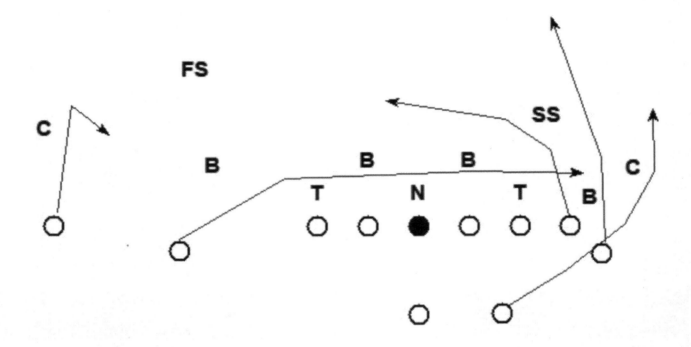

This is the Gun T version of Mesh-Rail. It is a simple progression for the QB. We want to throw the "F" on the Rail route if at all possible. We want to force the DB's and OLB's to our TE/Wing to pay for coming hard off the edge.

We read the corner on this concept. If he doesn't jump the Rail immediately, we throw that ball at about 8-12 yards. If he does jump the corner we look to throw the "B" on the skinny post as the TE should be holding the backside safety.

If the defense all drops into coverage and picks up both the deep routes, the "A" should be open on the crossing route.

Involving the Y

Involving the Y

This past season, we had a very talented Y on our roster. He was a solid blocker and was a very good receiving threat. While we have several base plays that make him an option, we wanted a few additional ways to highlight his skill set. The next section of this book will go over a few of the ways we involved him as a primary option catching the ball.

A few of the base plays that are not included in this book, but are in the other playbooks:

1) Waggle
2) Buck Pass
3) Trojan Pass

Most of the time on ANY play action, the Y will be the most likely to be open as those plays are designed to appear to the defense as a run and he will get lost.

Counter – Y Cross

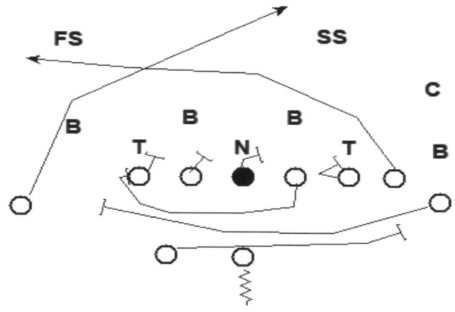

Position	Alignment
X	Skinny post – or "win" route (win inside)
A	Crossing route
F	Fake Counter and protect edge
Y	10-12 yard crossing route
B	Fake Counter and protect edge
QT	Rock or Load Protection
QG	Rock or Load Protection
C	Rock or Load Protection
SG	Rock or Load Protection
ST	Rock or Load Protection
Q	Keep ball behind back and read the corner

Counter Y-Cross

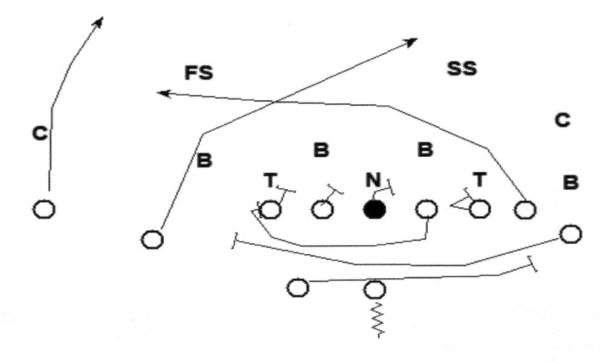

This is our play action off the counter play. The backfield action remains the same with the "F" and "B", or wing. They will simulate the double handoff look.

The strong guard will also pull in a "load" or "rock" protection. For the defense this looks similar to how we would block counter.

Our "A" works across the field and is not an option, but he must draw the attention of the safety. Our "X" work a win route or skinny post on the corner.

The "Y" works across the field at 10-12 yards depth.

The quarterback will put the ball behind his back and backpedal to buy time. He must hide the ball and allow the defense to read the counter action. While he backpedals, he is reading the corner. If the corner takes the "X" he will throw the "Y" on the crossing route. If he sits, he should be able to throw the "X" on the win route.

Buck - "Y" Peak

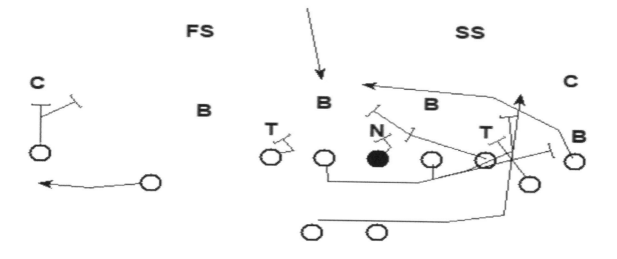

Position	Alignment
X	Auto off of run away
A	Auto off of run away
F	Buck
Y	Gap-down – PEAK – decide who runs the peak
B	Gap-down – PEAK – decide who runs the peak
QT	Buck Rules
QG	Buck Rules
C	Buck Rules
SG	Buck Rules
ST	Buck Rules
Q	Read the backside ILB

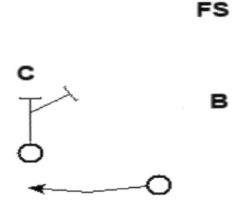
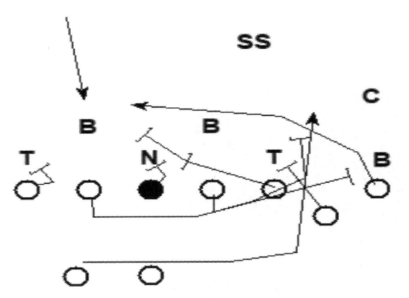

This has been a way to continue running our RPO game against either man-coverage or an OLB that will not allow our slot inside. It is a simple way to keep the same read for our QB as he would have on any of our "peak" concepts.

The "Y" and "B" must decide who is blocking the LB on the play as we will run either player on the "peak" route. This often depends on the defensive alignment.

The "peak" will be run a yard behind the LB. If he chases the guards the window will be very big to throw the ball.

This does take a little more time than our traditional "peak" look, so the QB may have to ride the mesh slightly longer.

Buck - "Y" Peak

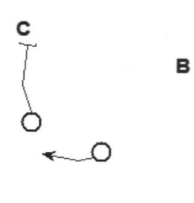

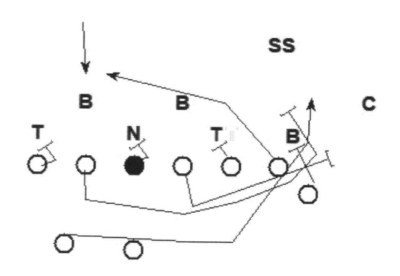

This is an example of the "Y" running the peak, due to the front of the defense. Because he is supposed to be going to the LB.

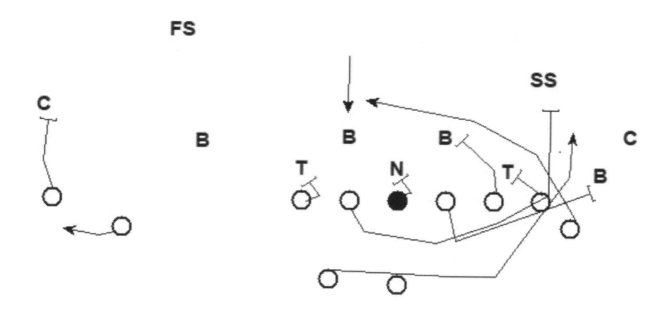

This is an example of our "B" running the peak, due to the front of the defense. In our offense our Strong Tackle would actually go down to the Nose before going up-field. If you do not teach that progression, you need a call so the ST does not go up-field on the RPO.

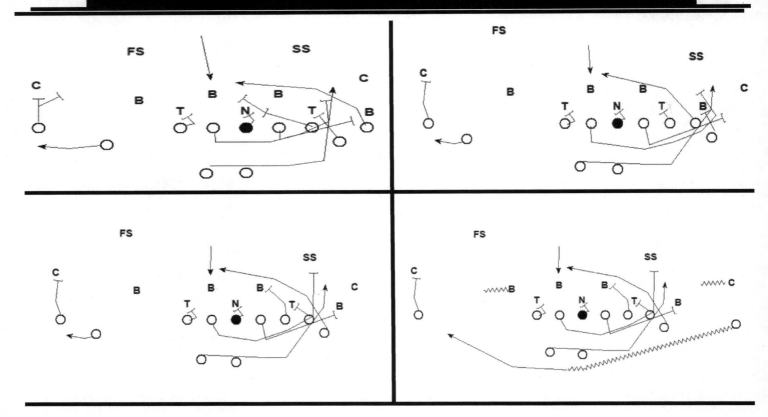

While there are more formations this can be run from, the basic premise is to run the RPO off Buck Sweep. We decide on who is running the "peak" based off the alignment of the defense and are comfortable to throw it to either player.

The aiming point of the "peak" route is the back hip of the player they would have blocked. QB must read it early and then buy a little time on the mesh to allow the player to cross.

Y Peak does need to be run off buck and only buck. While we would like to throw this ball, we don't want to end up giving it to a running back with unblocked defenders.

Buck - Y Peak

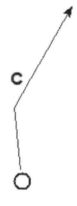

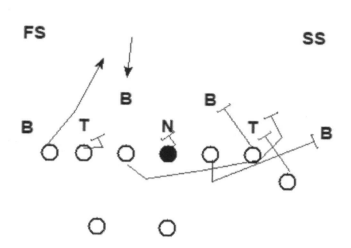

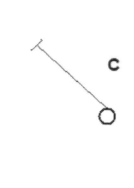

Position	Alignment
X	"Auto" or could block into the box
A	Skinny post or "win" route
F	Buck
Y	Peak route
B	Gap-down-backer
QT	Buck Rules
QG	Buck Rules
C	Buck Rules
SG	Buck Rules
ST	Buck Rules
Q	Read the backside ILB

Buck - Y Peak

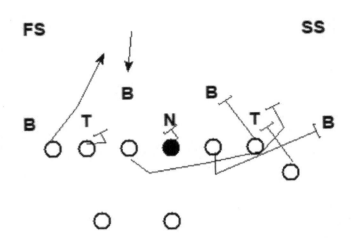

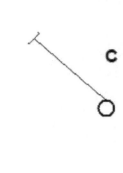

This is the exact same read for our QB out of our "Flop-Yo" set that forces the defense to balance to our offense.

The "Y" will run the peak route on the same ILB as he did from Red/Blue. The coaching point for him is that it needs to be a skinny vertical. Get head around quickly and be prepared to get hit after catching the ball.

The rest of the team is running our "Buck".

QB reads the same backside ILB as he does on all flavors of "peak".

*We can also run this RPO off of our Belly or Trojan play as it is a backside play.

Counter – Y Peak

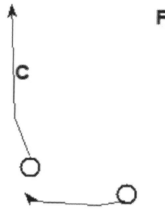

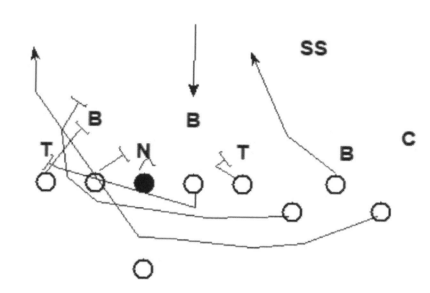

Position	Alignment
X	Go route
A	Running the counter
F	Bubble
Y	Run a skinny vertical – expect the ball at 7-12 yards
B	Pull wrap for counter
QT	Counter rules
QG	Counter rules
C	Counter rules
SG	Counter rules
ST	Counter rules
Q	Read the backside ILB for the Peak

Counter Y-Peak

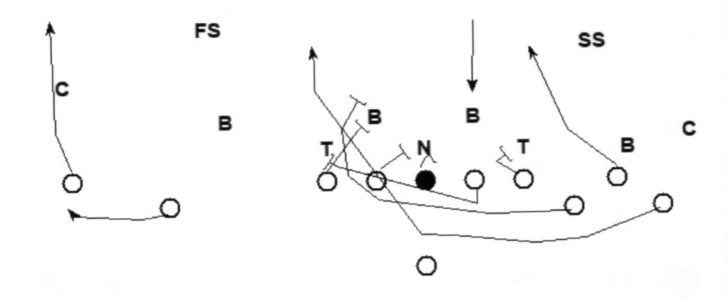

This is a way to involve the "Y" in the RPO game if the QB is able to read the mesh off our Counter play. We only run this from our "brown/black" type sets and from an empty look.

The pre-snap read is the bubble route from the slot (F) and the post-snap read is the backside ILB. If he chases the counter – we would throw the "Y" on the inside release.

50

Counter – Y Chute

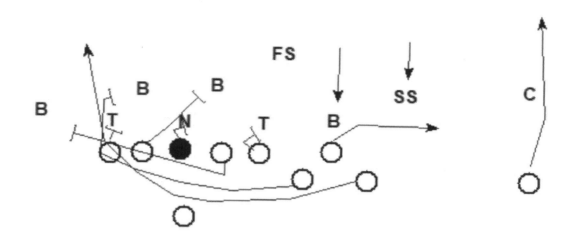

Position	Alignment
X	Go route
A	Running the counter
F	Outside Release – Go Route
Y	Chute Route
B	Pull wrap for counter
QT	Counter rules
QG	Counter rules
C	Counter rules
SG	Counter rules
ST	Counter rules
Q	Read the backside ILB for the Peak

Counter Y-Chute

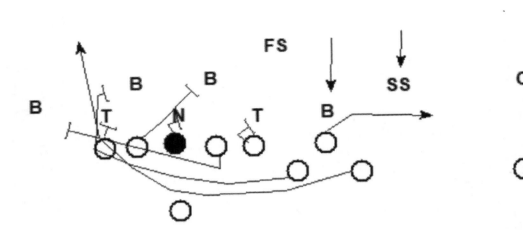

This is a way to involve the "Y" in the RPO game if the QB is able to read the mesh off our Counter play. He would read the backside force player for the "pull" read. Then the defensive back responsible for coverage second.

It is read very much like "steal" for the QB.

He would pull the ball to run first. Then flip the ball out the "Y" if the second read attacks.

*We have seen times that the defense only has only player outside the TE and have thrown it to him quickly.

Stick - Laser

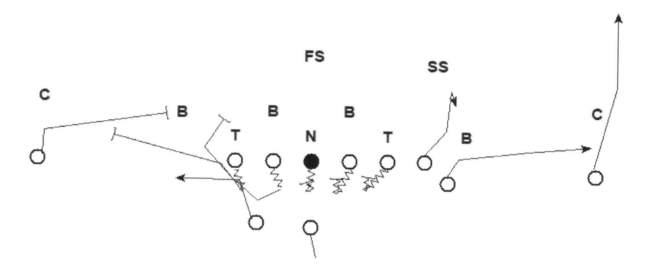

Position	Alignment
X	Can run off the corner, or crack the LB
A	Outside release, go route
F	Runs our "laser" screen – hide behind the line until the release
Y	Stick route – work to 8 yards and sit. Shuffle out if ball is not delivered.
B	Chute route
QT	Laser screen – Pass pro for a count, then work to force player/corner
QG	Laser screen – Pass pro for a count, then work to ILB
C	Pass pro
SG	Pass pro
ST	Pass pro
Q	Read the chute/stick on play side – if neither is open come back to screen

Stick - Laser

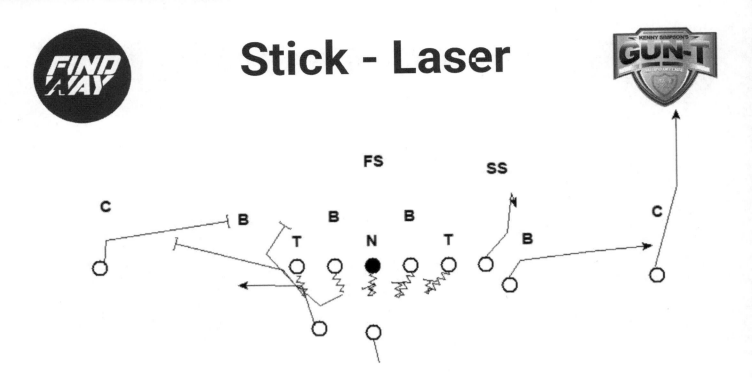

Simple concept for our team. We will read the overhang to the right. We want to throw the chute, but will come back to the TE on the stick route. If he is covered by the ILB, then we come back to the screen to the left.

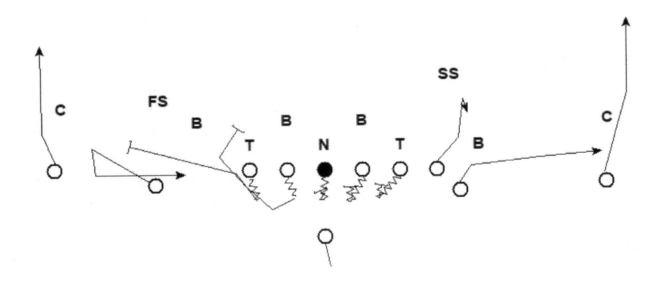

Same concept, but we are working from an empty set with he slot running the "laser" screen.

We could also do this with our "X" running the laser screen.

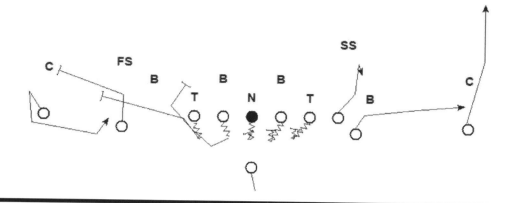

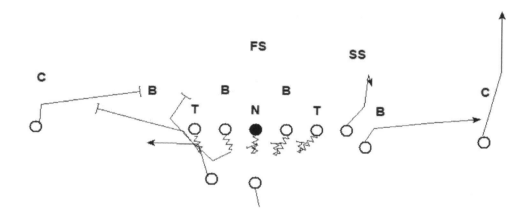

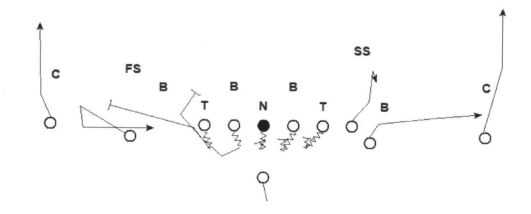

There are plenty of ways to run this concept, depending on who you want to get the ball to and how the defense is playing specific sets. Once the QB and OL learn the overall concept, the "tags" should be simple.

Brown – Buck Pass

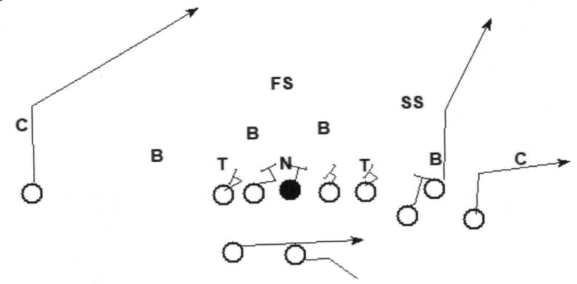

Position	Alignment
X	Post or "choice" route
A	Chute Route
F	Fake Buck
Y	Corner Route
B	Block Edge
QT	Rodeo/Lasso or Rock/Loa
QG	Rodeo/Lasso or Rock/Load
C	Rodeo/Lasso or Rock/Load
SG	Rodeo/Lasso or Rock/Load
ST	Rodeo/Lasso or Rock/Load
Q	Fake Buck – Read the Cornerback

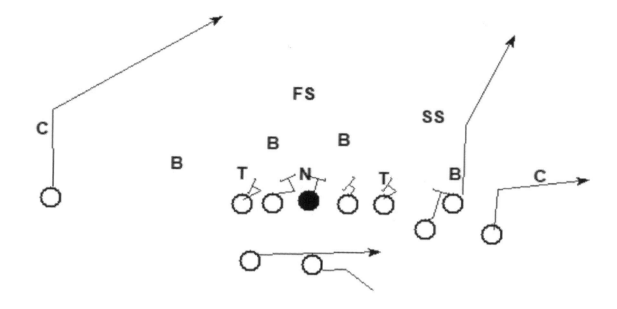

This is another way to run play action and involve our "A" or "Y" in a tight bunch look.

We can run a "Rock/Load" protection if the defense is reading the guards. In this example we are running "Rodeo" – which we would run against a stunting or undisciplined defense.

Our "Y" would run the corner route and our "A" is running a speed out (or chute).

The QB will ride the fake and read the Cornerback for the throw.

We can also run this same pass concept from a "strong" look with our "F" and roll the QB out.

Quick Game

In this offense, the ability to adapt to our personnel is key. The theory for us is to carry 3 base quick game concepts each season, but be willing to add more into the offense if we have the QB and WR's that will be a big factor in what we do. This past season we drew from the "Smash" world and some spread offenses.

It was given to us with the name "Connie" so we kept that same name, although each offense may have a "theme" for pass concepts, so feel free to name it what you'd like.

We ran this out of a rollout as our QB felt more comfortable with that, but it would work very well as a quick game concept.

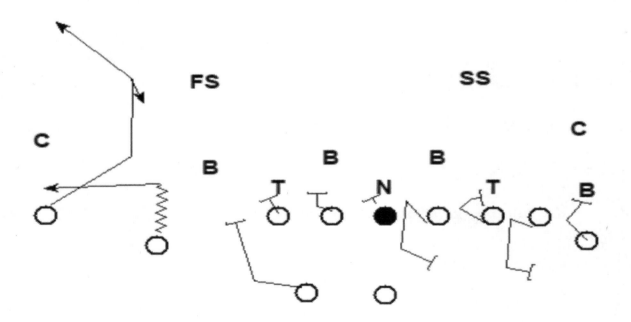

Connie

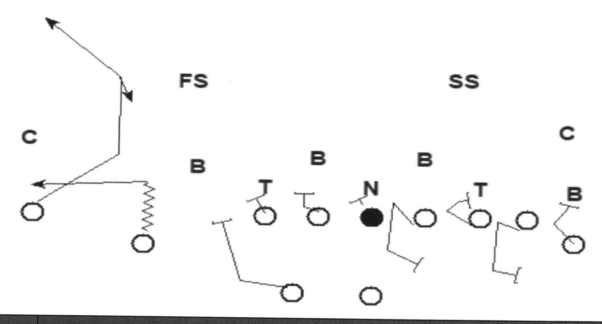

Position	Alignment
X	Runs 5 inside, 5 vertical – READ the corner – Either a corner or a curl
A	Slow off the ball and into a chute route
F	Rodeo/Lasso
Y	Rodeo/Lasso
B	Rodeo/Lasso
QT	Rodeo or Lasso Protection
QG	Rodeo or Lasso Protection
C	Rodeo or Lasso Protection
SG	Rodeo or Lasso Protection
ST	Rodeo or Lasso Protection
Q	Read the corner

Connie

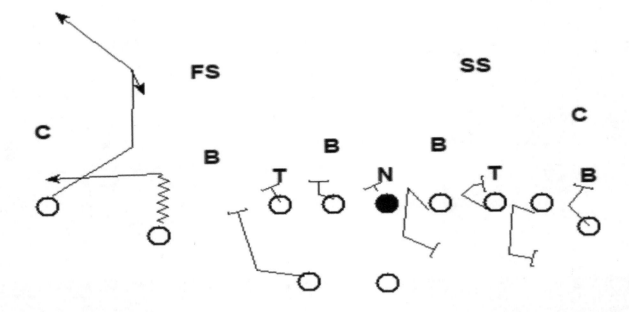

To us this is another way of running either smash or flat/curl. The defense makes the decision for us.

This is from a spread system – it is not something we came up with, but we love how it marries with our offense.

The "A" comes off the ball slowly and then runs a speed out route (almost like a chute).

The "X" will run 5 yards on the slant, 5 yards up-field and then read the corner. If he drops he will sit the route like a curl. If the corner bit on the out route he will run a corner route.

The QB reads the corner. If he bails we want to throw the out route quickly. If the overhang chases the out we can come back to the curl. If the corner jumps the out, we are going to throw the corner route.

Brown – F Rub

Position	Alignment
X	Post or Choice
A	Corner Route
F	Chute Route
Y	Block Edge
B	7 Yard – Hitch to Out
QT	Rodeo/Lasso
QG	Rodeo/Lasso
C	Rodeo/Lasso
SG	Rodeo/Lasso
ST	Rodeo/Lasso
Q	Read the Cornerback

F Rub

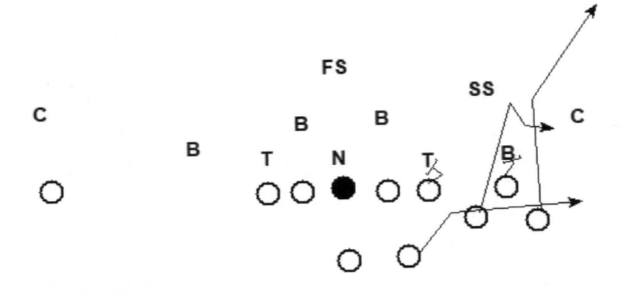

This is another concept we like to run against teams running man-to-man or attacking the bunch with the force player. We read the corner back for the throw and can come back to the "B".

The "Y" and the line will run Rodeo/Lasso.

Depending on our personnel, we could also give the "X" on the backside a route to run if we like that against man-to-man coverage.

Formations

Red

Position	Alignment
X	Top of the numbers
A	Split X and QT off the ball
F	Heels on QB toes. Split the QG and QT
Y	Head even with hip of center. 2 ft splits
B	2x2 off Y
QT	Head even with hip of center. 2 ft splits
QG	Head even with hip of center. 2 ft splits
C	On Ball
SG	Head even with hip of center. 2 ft splits
ST	Head even with hip of center. 2 ft splits
Q	Heels at 5 yards

Alignment

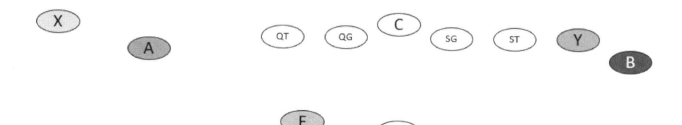

This is the 4.0 edition of this offense. Because of this, we will not go into every set we run, but the philosophy is simple:

1) Multiple formations – few concepts
2) Ability to tag formations with only a few key players moving
3) Use formations to create angles and mismatches

Throughout the rest of this book, we will be focusing on the newest formations tweaks and adjustments we have worked this season.

If you'd like to see all the books in this series:

OVER

Position	Alignment
X	On the ball to the "strong side" – Red = Right and Blue = Left
A	Off the ball to the "quick side"
F	Heels on toes of QB – Base rules apply
Y	Goes AWAY from the strong side
B	Goes TO the strong side
QT	Goes TO the strong side at the TE spot
QG	Normal rules
C	Normal rules
SG	Normal rules
ST	Normal rules
Q	Normal rules

OVER

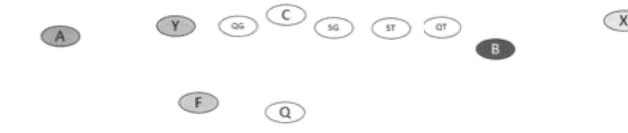

We have run "over" for several years, but this season our Quick Tackle was one of our best linemen and our "Y" was much more of a traditional Tight-End. This was an easy way to get our best blocker to the strong side, yet remain balanced to the DB's on the field as our "Y" had several catches.

With a quick shift or move, the "F" can make it an empty-trips look as well and cause issues for a defense to get aligned correctly.

Another potential benefit for this set is against man-to-man teams. Having our "Y" to the quick side will often draw another defensive back to cover on the backside. This could lead to better numbers to attack on the strong side.

We will run our entire run game (especially strong side) out of this set, for the sake of saving space in this book, we are only including our newer concepts we like off the backside.

Chute - RPO

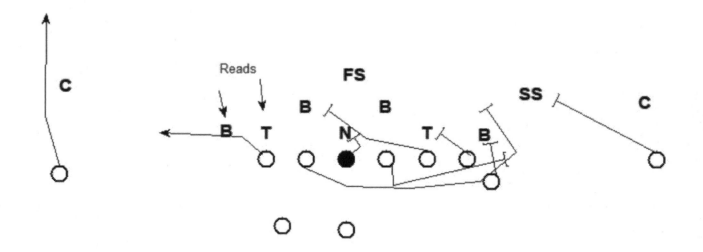

Position	Alignment
X	Base rules on run – crack or block corner
A	Outside release go route
F	Run called
Y	Chute route
B	Run called
QT	Run called
QG	Run called
C	Run called
SG	Run called
ST	Run called
Q	Reads backside like steal – the DL for pull and OLB/SS for throw

Chute - RPO

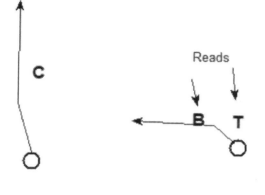

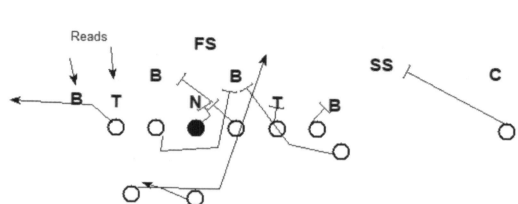

In our "Over" set we have an eligible TE on the quick side. On any of our base strong side runs we can run the "chute" RPO.

The QB will read this like steal with the defensive line. If they chase the guard we will pull the ball.

He then reads the force defender – if he covers the TE, he will run the ball. If he runs at the QB – we can throw the chute to the TE.

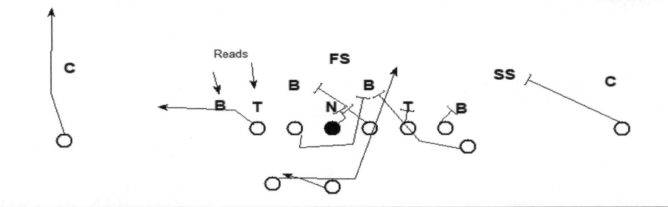

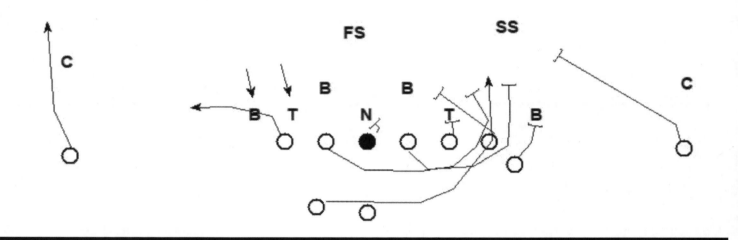

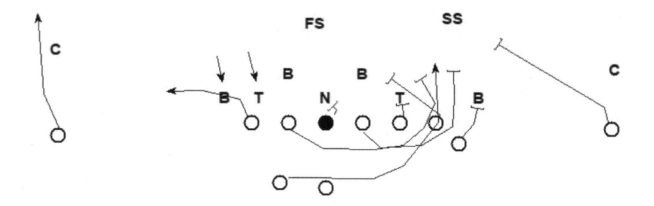

This RPO will work off any strong side run plays. Here is an example of it with our Belly, Buck and Trojan run plays.

Double -OVER

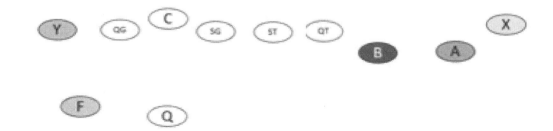

Position	Alignment
X	On the ball to the "strong side" – Red = Right and Blue = Left
A	Off the ball to the "strong side"
F	Heels on toes of QB – Base rules apply
Y	Goes AWAY from the strong side
B	Goes TO the strong side
QT	Goes TO the strong side at the TE spot
QG	Normal rules
C	Normal rules
SG	Normal rules
ST	Normal rules
Q	Normal rules

Double -OVER

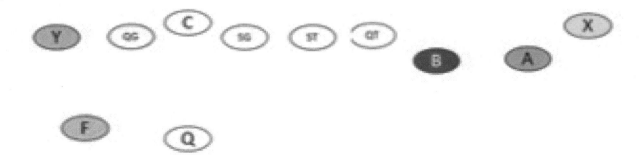

This is another way to get into an unbalanced look, but this time the offense has a trips set and unbalanced line to the strength. This set opens up the full run game and causes the defense to align to an over-set as well as a trips look to the right.

It can also open up the screen game to the X/A depending on the defenses' alignment.

On the backside the "Y" and "F" are both eligible as well.

We would run our full run game in this look as well, for the sake of space only a few are included.

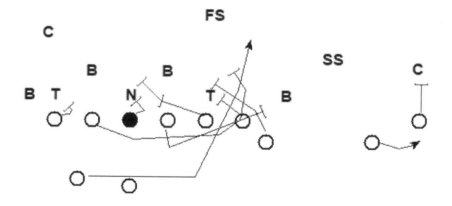

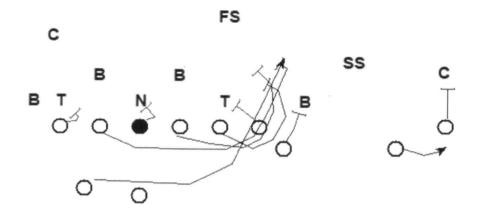

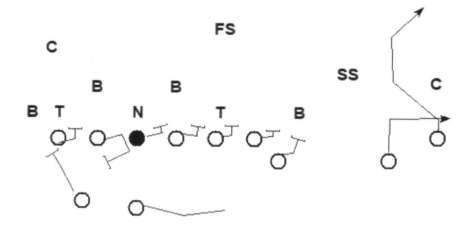

There are some base ways we would use this set. The first two are Buck and Trojan with a play side bubble route that can be thrown pre-snap. If the QB is advanced enough this can be thrown post-snap. We can also simply block with our WR's if we choose to do so. The bottom is a roll out quick game concept.

DBL Over - Connie

This is a roll out concept for our QB. Connie was covered in a previous section, but this is a good way to get to this look with a max protection for the QB as he reads the corner.

We could also run ANY roll out game concepts we like in this set.

FUNK

Position	Alignment
X	On the ball in the bunch trips – Prefer on the #s
A	Inside player in the bunch – 2 x 2 off the X
F	Outside player in the bunch – 2 x 2 off the X
Y	Backside at the tackle spot – he is eligible
B	2 x 2 off the QT (who is at the TE spot)
QT	Moves to an "over" look or at the TE spot
QG	Normal spot
C	Normal spot
SG	Normal spot
ST	Normal spot
Q	Normal spot

FUNK

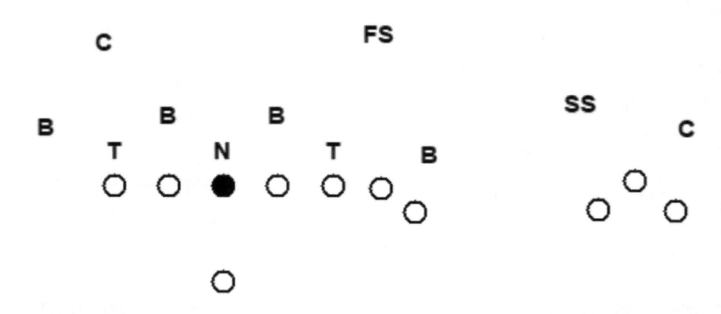

This has been another "unbalanced" look we have gone to with an athletic QB. We will move our "Y" to the quick side in this look and our QT over to the strong side. Our "X" is on the ball. Our "A" is the inside WR and the "F" is off the ball outside.

This causes the defense issues as they must decide ho to handle the trips and fit the run to the strong side. Because the "Y" is eligible on the backside.

This is a base look for a defensive front, but they could decide to play it much different.

The goal is simple for the Offensive Coordinator – find the numbers in the screen/passing game or run the ball. It will be difficult for the defense to account for both.

Funk Concepts

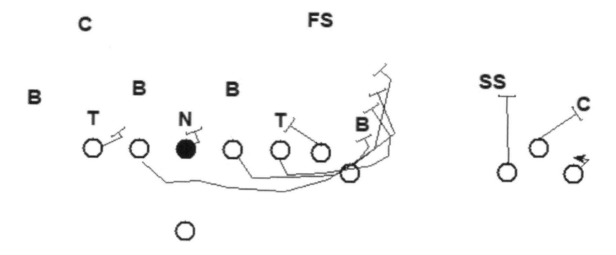

This is the first concept we work with our "Funk" look. A base run play – in this case "Trojan" – with a fast screen to our "F". This is usually a pre-snap read for us. It can turn into an RPO if the QB can read it on the run.

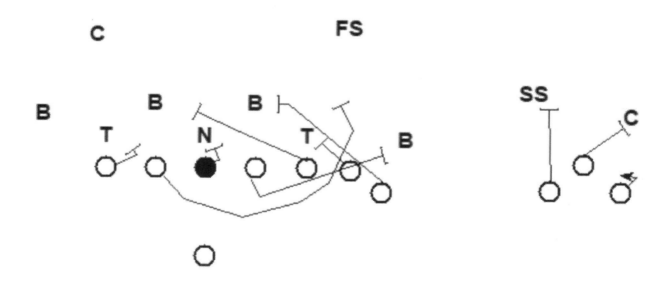

This is another example of a base run – Buck Sweep – paired with a fast screen to our "F". This is always a pre-snap read for us.

Trojan - Snag

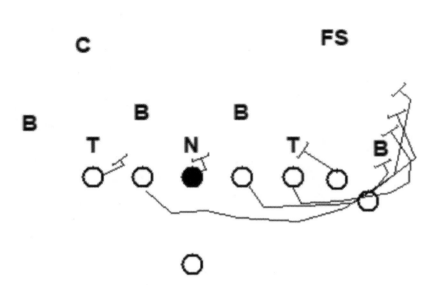

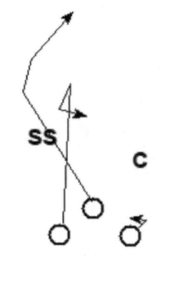

Another concept we run is our "Snag" concept with our bunch trips. In this scenario we would give an "alert" call to our offensive line to let them know not go downfield.

The QB has the option to run, but would read the corner for the "Snag" concept. We run this out of a "normal" trips look, so the read is familiar.

The "F" runs a fast screen. The "A" runs a 10-yard curl that can work to space. The "X" runs a post-corner route.

78

Counter Read

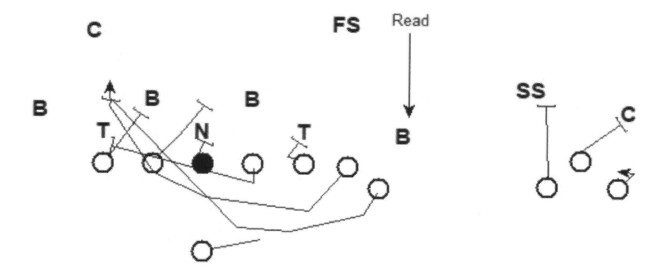

We will also run our "Counter-Read" concept from this look. The QB will read the force player for the pull option and can work to the fast screen PRE or POST snap.

We are blocking counter with our line and our bunch is working a fast screen.

Beast – DBL Over

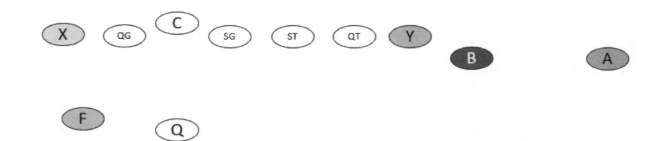

Position	Alignment
X	Usually this is a different player – but it can be same – lines up AWAY from strength
A	Off the ball – TO the strength call
F	Normal rules
Y	Normal rules
B	Normal rules
QT	TO the strong side. Aligns outside the ST.
QG	Normal rules
C	Normal rules
SG	Normal rules
ST	Normal rules
Q	Normal rules

Beast – Red DBL Over

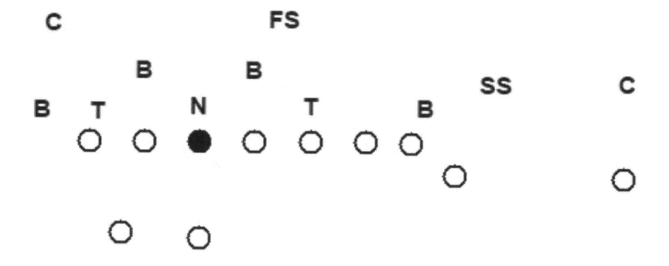

This has been a great "unbalanced" or "over" set for us out of our "Beast" personnel group. Usually, we will bring in another TE to play "X".

This alignment creates another gap on the strong side and can become very difficult to align to for the defense.

We will run all our base strong side runs from this set. The rules remain in place on Belly, Buck or Trojan.

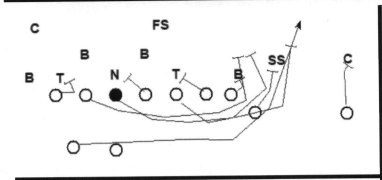

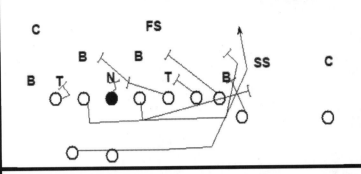

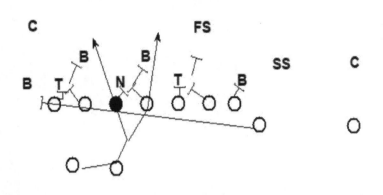

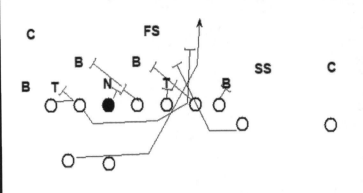

These are our base run plays from this set:

Top Left – Trojan

Top Right – Buck

Bottom Left – Duo

Bottom Right – Belly

As you can see, this set can help create an advantage in the run game to the strong side.

BEAST

Position	Alignment
X	Can be a personnel change – is at TE to the Quick Side
A	Off the ball – normal rules apply
F	Normal Position
Y	Normal Position
B	Normal Position
QT	Normal Position
QG	Normal Position
C	Normal Position
SG	Normal Position
ST	Normal Position
Q	Normal Position

BEAST

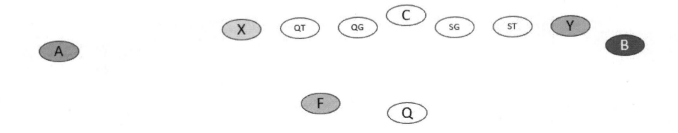

This is a set we started using often last season. It has helped us gain an additional gap for our offense and made it much more difficult team to overload our TE/Wing.

We can personnel our "X" with an additional TE if we feel we need to do so. It has been a great way to run the ball to the quick side as often defense will not account for each gap.

Orbit Motion

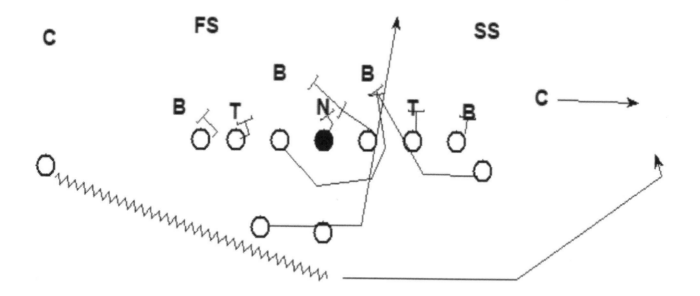

This is the a base play we run, with a motion from our "A" to help create space.

The orbit motion has been able to help us cause a rotation from the defensive backs.

The offense can run all base runs, with or without motion form this set.

Play Action

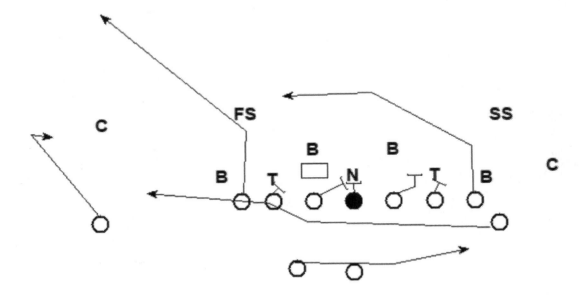

This is our Duo Pass.

In most offenses the TE is always open. And using the two TE set has allowed for us to create space for our players in the play action game.

We can also run our other play action passes from this same look.

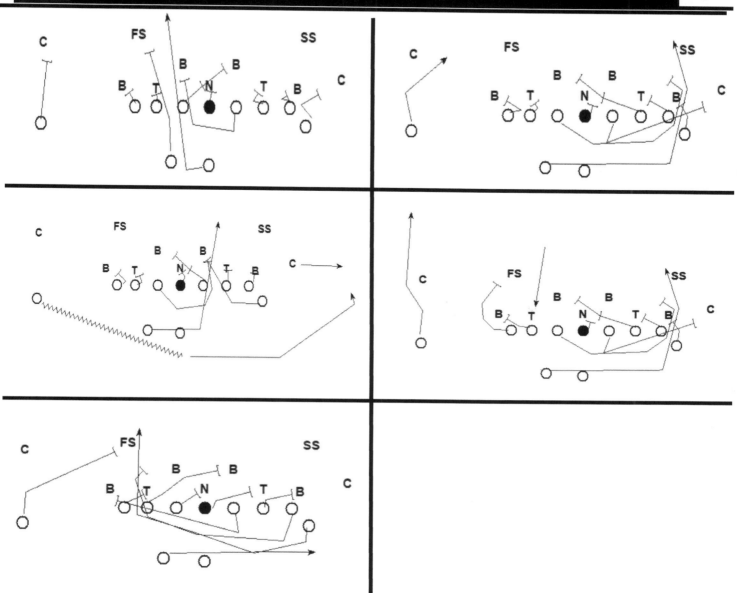

These are some other plays we would run from our "Beast" set. The goal is to take what the defense gives us.

The top left and bottom left are attacking the quick side.

The top right, and middle plays attack the strong side.

The middle right is our "steal" RPO we run with a TE.

Brown – Empty Strong

Position	Alignment
X	Base alignment – "Brown" = "Red" and "Black" = Blue
A	Outside WR in the tight bunch – 2 x 2 off the "B"
F	Off the ball – top of the numbers to the strength
Y	Off the ball – 2 x 2 off the ST
B	On the ball – 6-8' splits off the ST
QT	Base rules
QG	Base rules
C	Base rules
SG	Base rules
ST	Base rules
Q	Base rules

Empty sets in this offense are what can make a big difference. The defense will have to navigate through aligning to an "empty" and a "quads" and a "bunch" all while fitting the run game that the Gun T offers.

The base rules for runs do not change and the offense can attack the strong side or run counter back to the quick side as well as several options in the passing game.

Adjustment we can make due to personnel:

1) Switch the "Y" and the "B" – we would do this if the "B" was able to make the blocks required as the wing

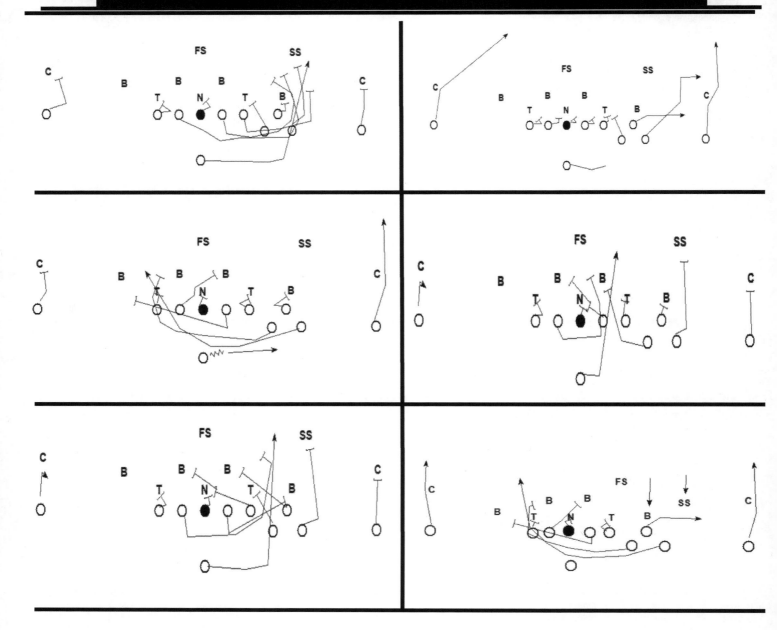

While we can run our entire offense from this set, here are 6 common plays we like from this set.

Top left – Q Trojan
Top right – Strong Flood
Middle left – Counter
Middle right – Q Belly
Bottom left – Q Buck
Bottom right – Counter – Y chute

Trojan

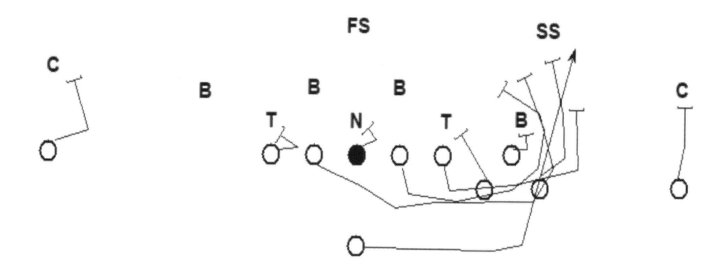

To keep our base rules the same on Trojan – we teach our "A" (outside in the bunch) to go to Safety.

Our Y/B block it the same as in all sets – block #1 and #2 – in this alignment it turns into a down block from wing.

Trojan has been a great play for us and this set is another way to run it well. I have it detailed in the 3.0 version here:

Belly

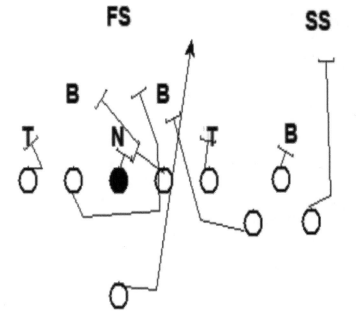

This is our version of belly from this set. We keep our rules the same – "A" goes to safety.

A great compliment to teams that may overload to stop the outside run.

We can also run any base strong side run in this set with our QB.

Counter – Y Chute

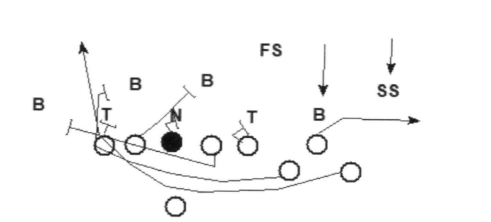

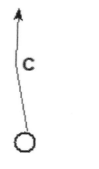

This is another way to involve our "Y" in the RPO game. We have paired this RPO with our "counter" play.

It is a read for the QB and a very good way to keep the defense honoring the strong side as the play attacks the quick side.

We can run the same play with no RPO if our QB is not a good RPO QB.

We can also run our "jet" series with our "A" if the defense shifts to the strong side.

Flood

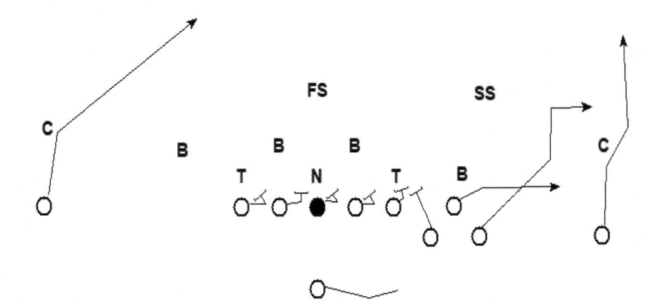

Simple way to run our flood concept. The QB has the "hot" read built in to the "Y" on the chute route if pressure comes off the edge.

If there is no pressure, QB will read the corner – most of the time we will throw the "smoke" route to our "A". This is our player that normally runs this route in our trips sets and is comfortable with the route.

We can also decide on a "choice" route to the backside "X" if the defense were to over-shift to the quads look.

Our "B" or if you personnel "Y" would seal the edge for the roll out for the QB. This can also set up a nice "throwback" option later in the game.

Heavy

Heavy

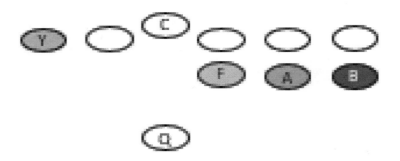

This is our base "Heavy" set. There are plenty of materials available about this set, but here are a few of the basics.

1) We generally snap to our best player and keep QB at "X" if he is not getting the ball

2) We will personnel our three up-backs with more physical players

3) Linemen will never pull, and we generally put our best lineman to the strength

Power-Pass

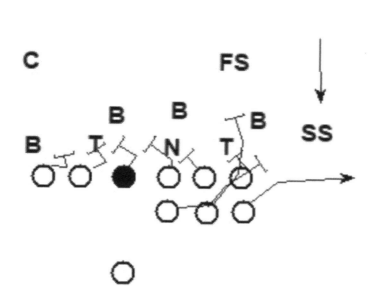

This is an RPO we have added to our "Heavy Package". Every player on the field blocks Power – except the outside up-man. He will run a chute route.

The QB will read the force defender.

If he attacks, we will throw the chute.

If he does not attack, we will run Power.

Outside WR must run a "Mandatory Outside Release" route.

Heavy - Over

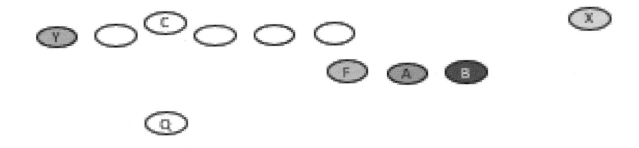

Position	Alignment
X	On the ball to the strength – This can be the QB if needed
A	Usually another player brought in – 2 x 2 off the end man
F	Usually another player brought in – behind the TE
Y	On the Quick Side
B	This can be another player brought in – 2 feet outside the "A"
QT	To the strong side at TE
QG	Normal Spot
C	Normal Spot
SG	Normal Spot
ST	Normal Spot
Q	This can be another player – usually our best athlete

Heavy - Over

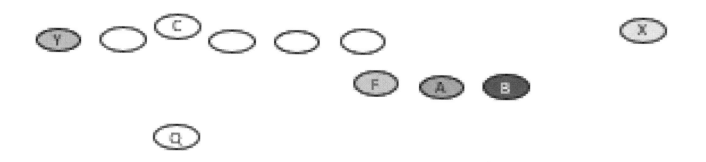

This has become a big adjustment for us in our "Heavy" package. We like to shift into this set.

The defenses have prepped for our base look and will overload the inside gaps. This look has allowed us to created an additional 2-gaps for the defense to cover.

While we can run our full series, we prefer to use this to run our "Trojan" or "Belly" play.

FORMATION

This is our belly play from this look. We would run this if the defense "over-shifts" or leaves a gap uncovered in the interior. Normal "belly rules" apply for the line. We would try to get two up-backs into the gap.

This is our trojan play from this look. We would reach #1 with our upback and block #2 with our second back. The 3rd up-back will read these blocks and turn up.

IF-THEN

IF - THEN

One of the parts of offensive system that have helped in calling plays or in solving issues within each concept has been the "IF-THEN" mindset. To understand what may be a problem and know what the adjustment will be before the game has been played. While this can be done with a full gameplan, it can also be done with as many concepts as possible.

In the following section, these are the basic "IF-THEN" for each run play in the System. I have also included a few blank sheets for each coach to write in their own "IF-THEN" charts.

Buck

This is our "Buck" IF-THEN chart. Our mindset on buck is to run it against any front at any time. In order for this to work, we must have answers to problems we will see from the defense. Buck can be an expensive play to install with many moving-parts. Because of this, we want to always have answers for what may be causing issues.

Below is our chart of answers.

IF	THEN	Notes
Backside ILB makes the tackle	Run "Key" or "Peak" RPO	Key – QB can run Peak – QB will throw
Backside 3 or 4 technique makes the tackle	Run "Steal" RPO	Want to pair this with bubble or a fast screen
Backside OLB is getting in box	Run Screen to Slot or Run the "Read" RPO	If man-to-man run the read concept
Having hard time blocking the 9 technique	Can run bypass and kick	Works for a defensive end that is getting penetration
The 9 technique is locking the TE	Have TE step to him and influence for 2 steps	Wing will seal him horizontally
The Nose Tackle is getting into gap and making the play	Have the strong tackle come all the way down to seal him	Shrink splits on strong side

Belly

This is our "Belly" IF-THEN chart. This is another run we feel should work against any defensive front. Belly is a play that should allow an offense to succeed even against a dominant defensive front, but there are a few issues that must be addressed.

Below is our potential answers to problems.

IF	THEN	Notes
Backside ILB makes the tackle	Run "Key" or "Peak" RPO	Key – QB can run Peak – QB will throw
Backside 3 or 4 technique makes the tackle	Run "Steal" RPO	Want to pair this with bubble or a fast screen
Backside OLB is getting in box	Run Screen to Slot or Run the "Read" RPO	If man-to-man run the read concept
The defense is in a 5-9-OLB	"Fan" call hit in B gap	Cheat Splits on strong side
The 9 technique is locking the TE	Cheat his splits or go "Flex"	
Play side LB is beating lead to make the tackle	Send play side OL directly to him and ignore DBL	

Quick Belly

This is our "Quick Belly" IF-THEN chart. This is a play we prefer against certain looks, but want to be able to run it against any front.

Below is our chart of potential answers to problems.

IF	THEN	Notes
Get a 5-3 Tech to the Quick Side	"Fan" call and run "A" gap	Widen splits to the play-side
Get a 4I and Nose	Can "Fan" block Can block down on 4I and hit C Gap	If fan call – widen split of QG
OLB is falling in on the tackle	Pair with RPO Run with Jet motion	If man-to-man use motion
Don't want to run with QB	Mustang Package "Same" side with RB	"Same" call – RB must cheat depth

Counter

This is our "Counter" IF-THEN chart. Counter is a play we can run a multitude of ways, but for this section, we are working with it being done from Red/Blue formations.

While there are many issues, we have listed the main 4 issues with counter and potential solutions.

IF	THEN	Notes
Play side DE is blowing up pull	"Lock" him with QT and double insert	Cheat Splits with QT on the 5-Tech
Backside DE is chasing down	Go Empty and Read him with QB	Better from "Flop" to pull the DB out
Issues with penetration on the play side	Shrink splits play side	
Wing miss cutback lane	Cheat wing deeper Take deeper counter step Pause longer	Most of the time wing is arriving too early to the hole

Jet

This is our "Jet" IF-THEN chart. Similar to Quick Belly, there are fronts we prefer this play against (usually slanting 3-4 or 5-2 looks), but we want to be able to run it against all looks.

Here are our answers to potential problems.

IF	THEN	Notes
Slower Player at "B"	Run to the boundary Run with "A" Run with QB	With "B" want to crack with WR's With QB run RPO
Slot cannot crack OLB	Expand and run Route	QB can read OLB
ILB making tackle	Run Quick Belly off fake	
Cannot reach the DE	Run Quick Belly Run Quick Belly Read	

IF - THEN

Here are a few blank IF-THEN charts to fill in for other concepts or issues you have faced or anticipate facing.

IF	THEN	Notes

IF	THEN	Notes

IF - THEN

Here are a few blank IF-THEN charts to fill in for other concepts or issues you have faced or anticipate facing.

IF	THEN	Notes

IF	THEN	Notes

New Wrinkles

New Wrinkles

O-Line Splits

This is not a new thing for us, but we focused more than ever on our "vertical alignment" as well as our normal "smart splits" with horizontal splits. Our offensive line was the smallest line we had ever had at our school and we made the move to the largest division we had ever played at this season. We needed every trick in the book to help create space.

Sugar Huddle

The use of a quick huddle has been around for a long time in multiple offensive systems. The Slot-T coaches use this every plays. We loved the use of this with our unbalanced sets and rule based blocking this season. This causes defenses more issues getting lined up and less time to find their keys.

One word "NASCAR"

We have always had this in our system. This season we went to 4 calls with our NASCAR package. Having the ability to take advantage of a defense after a big play or change of momentum has been a great addition to our offense.

Overview Alignment

While our offense is very much Wing-T based in it's run game, many of these concepts in this section should apply to many gap-scheme run attacks. We teach two types of alignment (or splits).

The first is "vertical" alignment. Or simply put, how close the lineman's helmet is to the line of scrimmage (or the ball before the snap). We NEVER want to cheat this alignment up. Gain as much space as possible off the line. This will clean up a multitude of issues:

1) Helps pullers and hides who is pulling
2) Helps slower lineman and eliminates stunts
3) Allows cut blocks to be much more effective
4) Creates much better angles for down blocking
5) Helps to eliminate as much penetration as the defensive line must now take multiple steps to make contact with the offensive line.

Vertical Alignment

This is an example of "vertical" alignment. We want our lineman to put their heads on the hip of the center. This helps with our angles and with our ability to pull in space.

If it is not coached, you will have issues getting pullers out into their lanes as they will need to gain even more depth. Another issue you may face will be that the guards will want to cheat deep, but the tackles cheat up. This will be a tendency the opponent will find if not addressed.

Vertical Alignment

This is a big visual of another reason we use "vertical alignment". We want to play physical football, but there are times that reality means we will give up penetration (as shown in the picture below). If we can seal players down, our pullers are able to get out and into the play. We ask our players to "block half a man" on all down blocks. By cheating our depth, we can handle this as well as quicker players.

Horizontal Alignment

This type of alignment we call our "horizontal" splits. We will adjust these season to season and even game to game or play to play.

While this may cause some tendencies, the defense does not have much time to pick up on them and the coach on the sideline cannot see this alignment well. These "cheats" have been very helpful for us as we often have very undersized linemen each week.

Feel free to adjust as needed, or do not cheat splits if you feel they are not needed by your players. We have always worked to give our players as many tools as possible to get the job done, and this has been a great addition.

General "rules" for these -
1) If we are pulling multiple players - cheat in
2) If we are running an inside run - cheat out
3) If we are double teaming - cheat together

Smart Splits Alignment

This would be an example of "smart" splits or cheating our splits with our line to create space.

We teach this with gap concepts or RPO game with the linemen to the point that they will understand how to use splits to help them. This goes along with teaching them the base concepts and what we are trying to accomplish with creating space with gaps, not upfield push. In the second picture we are running strong side belly.

Sugar Huddle

Sugar Huddle is not something that is unique to the Gun T System. But it is something that is a great weapon to add into the System. It has been used in the Wing-T system for years and is also used in the Slot T system.

The advantages for those using the Sugar Huddle are many:
1) The defense will have to identify the front quickly

2) Limits the defense's ability to stunt

3) Helps control the clock – can break the huddle at 8-seconds if desired

4) Another way to get plays into the offense without any "signal stealing"

5) Can force the defense to play a "right and left" and not a "strong side" look.

This is similar to going up-tempo in its effect on the defense. However, it allows the offense to control the clock and control the few looks the defense can give the offense. While it can limit RPO's (hard to know the alignment) and motions/shifts, the advantages often outweigh the disadvantages.

In order to be successful at running this look, an offense must practice this and be very disciplined in their rules. Often the defense will misalign to sets as they cannot get lined up properly. If the offense follows their blocking rules, this can be a great thing. But if the offensive linemen struggle with following rules, this could lead to missed assignments.

Sugar Huddle

This is an example of the sugar huddle in a game. The Center and WR's break on the first call. The rest of the offense is set behind the QB. On the second time the play is called, they will break and sprint into formation.

This is an example of breaking the huddle. We want to break the huddle and snap the ball within 3-4 seconds. This should cause the defense to play a balanced look (at least with personnel) as we will use unbalanced, balanced and normal formations from this huddle.

This is the offense getting lined up. The ball will be snapped very soon after this picture.

Sugar Huddle

The main rules for the Sugar Huddle

1) We send the center and any "receivers" – or detached players – after the first call

2) The rest of the players – usually 8-9 depending on the personnel group and formation – will break and snap the ball within 4 seconds of breaking the huddle

3) Linemen get into a 3-pt stance immediately

4) We rarely run motion from this look

The goal is to be able to get to the line and snap the ball before the defense can identify the front and run players to a "strong" and/or "weak" side. This should force them to play a "right/left" defense and allow us to dictate who we can run towards (or away from).

While we can run our full offense from the Sugar Huddle, the main sets we like from this look are the following:

1) Red/Blue (base)
2) Over sets – (TE to the quick side)
3) Heavy Package – We have started running our "Heavy" set to the left and right
4) Beast (2 TE package)

NASCAR

Our NASCAR package has been a mainstay the past three-seasons in the Gun T System. We usually pick the following plays –

1) A base run play
2) Another base run play
3) Play Action off a base run play
4) Fast screen to the perimeter

We teach it to be on the first sound. The line will get in a 3-point stance immediately on the call "NASCAR ___". Our line would be in our "Red" formation on each play. We taught our receivers they could line up in wherever they ended on the previous play, unless it was a play they needed to be lined up in "Red" – play action and/or screen.

This is practiced each day randomly throughout a team session so that our players are familiar with it.

Generally, a NASCAR play would be called after a first-down, or big play by the offense. The goal was to take advantage of the defense as quickly as possible with a base play we were comfortable with.

We also will run NASCAR "Freeze" or a check with me. This is any number not assigned to a play. For instance, this season we only had 4 NASCAR, so any number above 4 would be a "Freeze" call.

NASCAR

A few quick rules for NASCAR –

1)   We tell the receiver that unless it is a pass, they can align on either side of the ball and follow their automatics.
2)   The line will always be in "Red".
3)   We run this on first sound at the ball from a 2-pt stance with our linemen.
4)   No motions or shifts as we want to go as fast as possible

The idea on NASCAR is to run base plays that can be executed as fast as possible. The ability to change the tempo on a defense that is reeling due to a big play or change of momentum is big for any offense.

Conclusion

Conclusion

Each season an offense must adapt and adjust to how defenses are playing them. As a system that is becoming more widely known, this is a continual evolution of the Gun T. While the base plays will never change, the offense must have answers for potential problems a defense can pose.

It is my hope that as you learn this offense, you will add some of your own spin to it. Keep the base packages and take what will fit your athletes. Each season this offense can look "different" as it should have built in adjustments to highlight the talent on the team that season. Do not ignore the base concepts, but work hard to take some of these supplementary concepts that can help your team.

If I can do anything to help you in your journey as a coach, please do not hesitate to reach out.

My contact information: FBCoachSimpson@gmail.com

 # About the Author

Coach Simpson wrote his first book in 2019. He has since released 8 other books. *Find A Way: What I Wish I'd Known When I Became A Head Football Coach,* has been a three-time best seller on Amazon in several categories.

His offense has now run across the globe in not only the United States, but also in South America, Africa, Japan, Europe and Australia. He has helped to install the Gun-T system in many schools over the past 4-years.

Simpson has also raised over $1.5 million for Southside and has overseen several major facility projects including: New Field Turf, Expansion to Fieldhouse, Expansion to the school's home bleachers, and the addition of a press box and a new video-board.

Prior to coming to Southside, Simpson took over as Head Coach at Alabama Christian Academy in Montgomery, Alabama. During his tenure there, Simpson took over a team that had been 4-18 and led them to their first home playoff game in over 20-years. For his efforts he was named Montgomery Advertisers All-Metro Coach of the Year as well as being voted 4A Region 2 Coach of the Year (2010).

Simpson also served as the head track coach at ACA and led the girls' and boys' teams to multiple top 10 finishes in 4A.

Simpson began his coaching career at Madison Academy, in Huntsville, Alabama. He served as a junior high basketball and football coach, before working into a varsity coaching role in football. He graduated from Harding University in 2003. He is married to Jamey and has three children: Avery, Braden and Bennett. The couple was married in 2001 after meeting at Harding University.

 # About the Author

Simpson's Books

Find A Way: What I Wish I'd Known When I Became A Head Football Coach
Coaching Football Like A Basketball Coach
Training Athletes Beyond The Game
Athletic Fundraising
Team Themes
One Play Many Ways: Teaching Conceptual Football
Team Themes Volume 2
10 Hard Lessons Learned In Coaching

Gun T System Books

Gun T Playbook
Gun T 2.0
Gun T Organizational Manual
Gun T Offensive Line Manual
Gun T Youth Manual
Gun T 3.0
Gun T 4.0

Defensive Books

34 Fit and Swarm Overview
34 Fit and Swarm Organizational Manual

Made in the USA
Columbia, SC
07 November 2024

45657104R00070